Malcolm Hedding

The NEW TESTAMENT and ISRAEL

Biblical Zionism Series - Part 4

INTERNATIONAL CHRISTIAN EMBASSY JERUSALEM

The New Testament and Israel / Malcolm Hedding

ISBN 0-9765297-3-4

Copyright©2004 by:
International Christian Embassy Jerusalem – USA, Inc.
PO Box 39255, Washington, DC 20016

The International Christian Embassy Jerusalem was founded in 1980 as an act of comfort and solidarity with Israel and the Jewish people in their claim to Jerusalem.

From our headquarters in Jerusalem and through our branches and representatives in over 80 nations, we seek to challenge the church to take up its scriptural responsibilities towards the Jewish people, to remind Israel of the wonderful promises made to her in the Bible, and to be a source of practical assistance to all the people of the land of Israel.

All scriptures are taken from *The New King James Version.* 1996, c1982. Thomas Nelson: Nashville

CONTENTS

Israel's Call Is Irrevocable

The New Testament validates a number of things concerning Israel and the Jewish people, and the foundational scripture that sums it all up is Romans 11:28-29. In this scripture the Apostle Paul establishes the premise that God has never gone back on what He promised to the fathers concerning Israel.

This little passage is interesting because it concedes Israel's rejection of the Messiah, but nevertheless affirms that whatever promises God has made to Israel through the fathers remain intact. In light of this passage it is difficult to understand how some segments of the church today disinvest Israel of a national destiny in the land of Israel. So let us look at what it says:

> [28] Concerning the gospel they are enemies for your sake, but concerning the election they are beloved for the sake of the fathers. [29] For the gifts and the calling of God are irrevocable.
> *(Romans 11:28-29)*

God's plan of calling Israel into existence to be the vehicle of world redemption has never changed. Verse 29 says that once God calls a people into a peculiar role in history, He does not go back on that.

According to the New Testament, God has not gone back on His promises to Israel that were clearly given in the Abrahamic covenant. This little passage alone ends the debate about Israel and her destiny.

Israel must be restored to her ancient homeland and continues to serve the purposes of God in that regard. This part of the Word of God is therefore crucial and foundational to our study.

The Coming Kingdom

The New Testament validates the Old Testament concept of kingdom. Jesus' words, while upbraiding His generation for their apostasy and unbelief, constantly affirmed the notion of a coming kingdom that will reign over the earth from Jerusalem. We see that in Acts:

> ⁶ Therefore, when they had come together, they asked Him, saying, "Lord, will You at this time restore the kingdom to Israel?" *(Acts 1:6)*

The disciples knew that He was about to be taken from them into heaven to be seated at the right hand of God, and so they popped the question that was burning in their hearts: "Lord, will You at this time restore the kingdom to Israel?" And He said to them:

> ⁷ ..."It is not for you to know times or seasons which the Father has put in His own authority. ⁸ But you shall receive power when the Holy Spirit has come upon you; and you shall be witnesses to Me in Jerusalem, and in all Judea and Samaria, and to the end of the earth." *(Acts 1:7-8)*

Jesus does not deny that the kingdom will be restored to Israel. He merely says it is not for them to know when this will happen. So here the New Testament clearly validates the concept of a coming kingdom.

In addition, we have the episode of Jesus recorded in Matthew 23 where He weeps over Jerusalem and depicts the city as a people. It is clear that when speaking to Jerusalem here, He is speaking to the Jewish people.

> [37] "O Jerusalem, Jerusalem, the one who kills the prophets and stones those who are sent to her! How often I wanted to gather your children together, as a hen gathers her chicks under *her* wings, but you were not willing! [38] See! Your house is left to you desolate; [39] for I say to you, you shall see Me no more till you say, *'Blessed is He who comes in the name of the LORD!'"*
>
> *(Matthew 23:37-39)*

What He says here is that Jerusalem, meaning the Jewish people, must welcome Him back in order to see Him again. The fact that He speaks to Jerusalem and personifies it means that He is speaking to the people of Israel. It is then clear that they have to be back in their land at some point in order to welcome Him back. Therefore, Jesus presupposes a restoration of the Jewish people to their historical homeland so that He can come and usher in His kingdom.

That is very important because it is the same Jesus who in other passages of the Gospels (Matthew 24, Mark 13, and Luke 21) speaks about the dispersion of the Jewish people to the four corners of the earth.

8

Luke 21 is an interesting passage in this regard because here the Lord Jesus takes the whole sweep of Jewish history into account. I do not have to tell you that the twenty-first chapter of Luke is an eschatological chapter. That is, He is talking about the signs that will take place just before His coming. This chapter is repeated, as I have just stated, in Matthew 24 and Mark 13.

In Luke 21, He speaks about the signs that will precede His coming - the signs His followers should look for. He talks about the Jewish people and He says:

> ^{24} "And they will fall by the edge of the sword, and be led away captive into all nations. And Jerusalem will be trampled by Gentiles until the times of the Gentiles are fulfilled." *(Luke 21:24)*

So here, Jesus Himself speaks about a dispersion of the Jewish people. He speaks about the city of Jerusalem being occupied and held underfoot by great Gentile nations. We who have hindsight in our favor can now see how that has happened exactly as He said. Jesus was a true prophet.

However, in the same passage He also clearly talks about the removal of Gentile ascendancy over Jerusalem. This can only mean the restoration of the Jewish people to the city. This is one of the great events that has to go into the basket of end time signs.

It is a remarkable prophecy, because in our day we have seen the fulfillment of it. It is not something we look at and wonder about anymore because we can open our Bibles and we can look at the city of Jerusalem and we can see that the Jewish people have returned to it. They are now in control of it, for the first time in over 2,000 years.

Just an aside here - the "times of the Gentiles" in this verse must be distinguished from what Paul called the "fullness of the Gentiles" in Romans 11:25. The fullness of the Gentiles has to do with the full number of Gentiles throughout the nations who will accept Jesus Christ as their Lord and Savior.

But here in Luke 21:24 the times of the Gentiles has to do with the ascendancy of the Gentile nations over Israel. It is a subject that is dealt with in detail by the prophet Daniel.

Jesus clearly states in Luke 21:24 that there will be a time when the Gentiles will no longer rule Jerusalem, and therefore Israel will have returned to her ancient homeland. This return will be a preparation for His coming kingdom. It is important for us to understand this.

The events that surround the consummation of history as we know it are always seen against the backdrop of a restored Jewish nation. This is the conclusion that we make from these statements of Jesus.

In Matthew 19, for instance, there was a little debate raging amongst the disciples. They had given up everything to follow Jesus and wanted to know what they were going to get out of this. Human nature is always the same, is it not? What do I get out of this? Jesus, in a very loving way, replies to Peter. But notice His language:

²⁷ Then Peter answered and said to Him, "See, we have left all and followed You. Therefore what shall we have?"

²⁸ So Jesus said to them, "Assuredly I say to you, that in the regeneration, when the Son of Man sits on the throne of His glory, you who have followed Me will also sit on twelve thrones, judging the twelve tribes of Israel…"

(Matthew 19:27-28)

So here again we have this remarkable picture of a Jewish kingdom and a Jewish King sitting on His throne.

He uses the term "regeneration," which conveys the thought that something is improved. So it is quite clear that He is talking about this world. He is not talking about the eternal state or the New Jerusalem that we see pictured at the end of the book of Revelation. This perfect eternal "world" does not need improvement!

He is talking about this earth that is regenerated or improved when He comes again. The Bible gives us a wonderful picture of this regeneration because it says that even the natural order, including that of the animal kingdom, will be changed in the messianic age. Lions will not be flesh-eaters anymore and the lion and the lamb will lie down together. There will be a significant disposition change in the natural kingdom (Isaiah 11:6-9).

The Apostle Paul in the book of Romans also talks about this regeneration of the earth. The earth is laboring or groaning because it is longing to be delivered from its present futility into the glorious liberty of the children of God. In other words, when the children of God are resurrected and finally find themselves perfect, in the presence of God in this messianic age, then the earth itself will be resurrected. It will undergo a metamorphosis. It will be regenerated and improved.

If we think the earth is beautiful now – its natural vestiges of valleys and splendor – it is nothing compared to what will happen when Jesus puts His feet on the Mount of Olives. The world is going to undergo a metamorphosis.

> [18] For I consider that the sufferings of this present time are not worthy *to be compared* with the glory which shall be revealed in us. [19] For the earnest expectation of the creation eagerly waits for the revealing of the sons of God. [20] For the creation was subjected to futility, not willingly, but because of Him who subjected *it* in hope; [21] because the creation itself also will be delivered from the bondage of corruption into the glorious liberty of the children of God. [22] For we know that the whole creation groans and labors with birth pangs together until now.
>
> *(Romans 8:18-22)*

This clearly teaches that there is a kingdom coming that will regenerate the present creation and that will be the kingdom of the Son of David when He reigns from Jerusalem. The New Testament strongly endorses that concept.

The details that have to do with the consummation of the age – that are the precursor to this incredible day – all assume a backdrop of a restored Jewish nation.

They will be the ones to invite the King back and they will not see Him again until they do so.

> [39] "for I say to you, you shall see Me no more till you say, *'Blessed* is *He who comes in the name of the* LORD!'"   *(Matthew 23:39)*

Talking to a personified Jerusalem, that is, as we have seen, the Jewish people, He says that there will be a day at the consummation of the age when they will bring Him back. Again, I stress this implies that there must be a restored Jewish presence in Jerusalem for this to happen.

The New Testament validates the Old Testament concept of a coming kingdom. How wonderful to know that the creative order that we interact with and enjoy every day – the trees, animals, and birds, etc. – will be regenerated. In the light of global warming and mankind's abuse of his environment, this is encouraging.

The Bible says there is going to be a regeneration of the world and the natural world will undergo a climatic change the likes of which we cannot fully appreciate. It is going to be an extraordinary time...and the Old Testament concept of a literal kingdom with the Son of David seated on the throne is confirmed by the new covenant scriptures. All of this is linked to a restored Jewish nation in the land of her forefathers.

The Historical Mission of Israel

We established earlier from Romans 11:29 that God has called the Jewish people into a peculiar role. About this He has never changed His mind. He has never replaced them, and the unique call or mission that He gave them in history has never been removed from over their national life.

It is important for us to understand that the New Testament completely undergirds the notion that the nation of Israel constitutes God's vehicle of world redemption. The wonderful thing about this is that God has used Israel's belief and her unbelief to achieve His purpose. He used her as a vehicle because He chose her! This choice had nothing to do with her salvation.

Of course God loves her and wants her to be saved and she has had every opportunity in this regard, but His choice of her as a nation had nothing to do with her salvation. She became the vehicle of world redemption. That is, the means by which He would bring His great message of salvation to a lost world. In accomplishing this He has used her belief and her unbelief.

She served the world by virtue of her unbelief by giving to the world the death of Jesus. She took Him to the cross, and she crucified Him but she did it in ignorance (Acts 2:22; 3:11-18; 5:30; 7:52; 10:39). The Jewish people are not Christ killers. They are not guilty

15

of deicide. They are not under a generational curse nor do they deserve to be hounded throughout history. That is evil and we have to stand against all forms of anti-Semitism.

The fascinating thing is that God did use her unbelief as well as her belief to bless the world. It is through great Jewish prophets and men of God that we have the Bible. These were men who loved God and who served Him, and they were saved. They were saved by looking forward to the cross.

No one in history ever got saved by any other means than the death of Jesus. You must understand that. They looked forward to the cross. Therefore, even if they only understood the shadow of it, or understood something of the essence of it but had faith in God, then they were saved on the basis of it. Abraham believed God and it was accounted to him for righteousness.

Our generation looks back to the cross. We have a greater privilege because we know its fullness and we therefore have no excuse. Neither do the Jewish people have an excuse because they also look back.

So you have great biblical prophets who gave us the Bible and who prophetically saw the death of Jesus. In Psalm 22 David writes of Jesus' death as does Isaiah in chapter 53. Abraham, according to the new covenant, saw the day of Jesus' death and rejoiced in it (John 8:56).

We also have the testimony of Job. The book of Job is a mystical book and a very interesting one. Sometimes we do not understand it as we should because the advice of his friends was actually good advice. It was just given at the wrong time and to the wrong guy! In other words, they gave advice without wisdom. What is wisdom according to the Bible? Wisdom is the ability to apply knowledge correctly.

So, the book of Job should interest you because you might be the right guy. In other words the advice that Job's friends gave just might apply to your circumstances and from time to time it does. So read the book with expectation. That is the lesson; it is a question of timing and wisdom.

Job's friends are telling him that the reason he is full of boils and funny sicknesses and has scales all over his head, and the reason he is sitting in a hump in the corner, is that he has sinned and God is judging him. Job defends his integrity and says, "No way, no way, I know that I have not sinned." And then Job makes this wonderful statement in the midst of his suffering:

> [25] For I know *that* my Redeemer lives,
> And He shall stand at last on the earth....
> *(Job 19:25)*

Job could look forward and see with remarkable clarity the purpose of God in His Messiah. That is truly amazing. This fact was his hope and expectation.

So the Jewish people gave us this book by their belief. Then, however, in the fullness of time they passed into unbelief and they gave us our Messiah. He died upon the cross and opened up a wellspring of salvation, so that we could be washed from our sins and have eternal life. This is the remarkable teaching of the

New Testament. It validates the historical mission of the nation of Israel. Jesus, of course, affirmed this when He said, "salvation is of the Jews" (John 4:22).

In Romans 3 Paul says the chief purpose of the Jewish people, as an elected group of people for a special mission, is to be the custodians of the Word of God. The book of Revelation, on the other hand, pictures Israel as the pregnant woman; the imagery comes from the thirty-seventh chapter of the book of Genesis. Her mission is to bring truth into the world to bring God's redemptive purpose to a world fallen in sin, and that culminates with the arrival of the male Child (Revelation 12:5,13).

In Romans 11, however, we find that the Apostle Paul speaks about Israel's unbelief and tells us that Israel's unbelief has served the nations.

> [28] Concerning the gospel they are enemies for your sake, but concerning the election they are beloved for the sake of the fathers. [29] For the gifts and the calling of God are irrevocable.
> *(Romans 11:28-29)*

It is hard to understand that they are our enemies for the sake of the gospel, but concerning the election, that is, God's mission bequeathed to them as the custodians of God's redemptive purpose for the world, they are beloved for the sake of the fathers. For the gifts and calling of God are irrevocable.

Now let us read from verse 11 of that great chapter:

> [11] I say then, have they stumbled that they should fall? Certainly not! But through their fall,

to provoke them to jealousy, salvation *has come*
to the Gentiles. [12] Now if their fall *is* riches for
the world, and their failure riches for the
Gentiles, how much more their fullness! [13] For I
speak to you Gentiles; inasmuch as I am an
apostle to the Gentiles, I magnify my ministry,
[14] if by any means I may provoke to jealousy
those who are my flesh and save some of them.
(Romans 11:11-14)

So their unbelief has served the purposes of God.
Here he concedes that Israel's rejection of Jesus'
messianic credentials served the purposes of God for
reaching the Gentile world. There is an element of
mystery in that. We can only thank God that through
the nation of Israel we have had an opportunity to hear
about this wonderful Messiah who has saved us and
caused us to be born again, has changed our lives and
given us an eternal hope - a hope that does not fade
away.

So again, this passage validates the historical
mission of the nation of Israel. It in no way removes
her mission; in fact, it gives added meaning to it – that
the nation of Israel has served the world by her unbelief
and by her belief.

So we thank God for Israel because we understand,
as we have seen in these studies, that a Jew is a Gentile
brought into a peculiar relationship with God for the
purpose of world redemption. How we thank God that
He took the initiative and called Abraham.

He demonstrated in her patriarchs what He was
going to do. In Abraham He promised the world eternal

life, in Isaac He promised the world atonement, and in Jacob He promised the world transformation.

It is clear then that the New Testament validates the historical mission of the nation of Israel. Romans 9 underlines the same truth.

> [3] For I could wish that I myself were accursed from Christ for my brethren, my countrymen according to the flesh,
> [4] who are Israelites, to whom *pertain* the adoption, the glory, the covenants, the giving of the law, the service *of God,* and the promises;
> [5] of whom *are* the fathers and from whom, according to the flesh, Christ *came,* who is over all, *the* eternally blessed God. Amen.
>
> *(Romans 9:3-5)*

The Apostle Paul here rams home this point with great clarity when he says that the Jewish people have given us everything – the adoption, the glory, the covenants, the giving of the law, the service of God, the promises, and our Messiah, Christ Jesus!

In short, the New Testament validates the historical mission of the nation of Israel to be the vehicle of world redemption.

Affirmation of the Abrahamic Covenant

The Abrahamic covenant guarantees a national destiny for the Jewish people in the land of Canaan. This is because God needed a nation by which to reach the world with His love.

A nation can only be established on a land. Land gives a nation soul, character and continuity. He needed a people and He gave them a small piece of land in the center of the earth. The Word of God says that the land of Israel is situated at the very center of the earth (Ezekiel 5:5). From this center His plan will radiate to the four corners of the earth.

So the Abrahamic covenant is the covenant of God's decision to save the world. "In you all the families of the earth will be blessed" (Genesis 12:3).

But it is also the covenant that brings into existence the vehicle of world redemption: the Jewish people. They will be the servants of this covenant. I always liken it to the celebration of Hanukkah. Hanukkah is the Feast of Dedication that is mentioned in the Gospel according to John (John 10:22). It celebrates the miraculous rededication of the temple under the Maccabees.

The story begins around 168 B.C. when the Hasmonean family, otherwise known as the Maccabees ("the Hammers"), revolted against Antiochus Epiphanes, who was the ruler over the region from Syria down through the Middle East. He was a Grecian and wanted to Hellenize the world. In order to Hellenize the land of Israel he needed to eradicate the worship and the religion of the Jews.

This is the "vulture" again seeking to liquidate the Jewish people and to destroy them. He came into the Holy Land and defiled the temple and set up an altar to Zeus. Thus, the first Antichrist was actually Antiochus Epiphanes, which means "the shining one." He is the prototype and he is the picture of Antichrist that Jesus and Paul both picked up on because he committed the abomination of desolation.

So the Maccabees revolted against him. They were a deeply religious family and resented this intrusion and attempt to liquidate the Jewish people and their way of worship. Their revolt began at a village called Modi'in which is near today's Ben Gurion Airport.

After the Maccabees defeated Antiochus, they began to clean and rededicate the temple in Jerusalem. As they reinstated all of the various aspects of worship in the temple, they needed to rededicate the menorah, which is the seven-branch candelabra that burns in the temple continually. Sadly, they only had sufficient oil for one day. To get more oil they had to go to the Galilee, which took four travel days there and four days back.

God honored their efforts to reestablish the temple and a miracle happened. The oil that was only sufficient for one day burned for eight days until the new oil arrived. So they could continue to have the light of the presence of God symbolized by the candelabra burning in the temple. Now Jesus celebrated this miracle and therefore validated it.

The interesting thing about the candelabra used to celebrate Hanukkah is that it is an eight-branch candelabra because of the eight days. There is, however, also a ninth branch, which is hidden behind it. The ninth branch is the "helper," or "servant," as it is used to light all the other branches. This is what Israel has done for the world. She has been God's servant to spread His shining light from one nation to the next – even to where you live.

So how did the grace of God come here? Because of a little helper that you cannot see that has lit up everything. That is the role of Israel historically and this is validated by the Abrahamic covenant.

The New Testament clearly enforces and undergirds the Abrahamic covenant. It strengthens the covenant and even holds it up as an example of God's faithfulness. For 4,000 years He has kept His covenant with us to save the world and to use Israel as the vehicle of world redemption.

This constitutes a big problem for "replacement theologians" because they in fact say that the Abrahamic covenant is annulled. If that is the case, then what the New Testament has to say about the Abrahamic covenant has to be a lie. Of course, we know it is not.

God has never changed His mind about the Jewish people, and the New Testament undergirds that. In the book of Hebrews, for example, the writer holds up the Abrahamic covenant as a symbol of God's faithfulness.

We know that we can trust Him in terms of everything He said to us about Jesus, about what He would do in our lives, because He gave His promise to Abraham. He swore by His character. He has never changed His mind and therefore we can confidently serve this God and love Him because He is faithful.

> [13] For when God made a promise to Abraham, because He could swear by no one greater, He swore by Himself, [14] saying, *"Surely blessing I will bless you, and multiplying I will multiply you."* [15] And so, after he had patiently endured, he obtained the promise. [16] For men indeed swear by the greater, and an oath for confirmation *is* for them an end of all dispute. [17] Thus God, determining to show more abundantly to the heirs of promise the immutability of His counsel, confirmed *it* by an oath, [18] that by two immutable things, in which it *is* impossible for God to lie, we might have strong consolation, who have fled for refuge to lay hold of the hope set before *us.*
>
> *(Hebrews 6:13-18)*

This passage teaches us that He has not changed His mind about Israel, as the vehicle of world redemption, and He has not changed His mind about saving you in Jesus. You can trust Him forever with your life, with your circumstances, with your property, with every part of what you are. You can trust this God. Why?

Because all the promises He made in the Abrahamic covenant, He has kept!

[19] This *hope* we have as an anchor of the soul, both sure and steadfast, and which enters the Presence *behind* the veil, [20] where the forerunner has entered for us, *even* Jesus, having become High Priest forever according to the order of Melchizedek. *(Hebrew 6:19-20)*

It is clear that Jesus came in fulfillment of the Abrahamic covenant. We see this truth in Luke 1 where Zacharias thanks God for His faithfulness in sending John, the forerunner, who will pave the way for the Messiah. He says that all this has happened because God is faithful to His Abrahamic covenant.

[71] "That we should be saved from our enemies
And from the hand of all who hate us,
[72] To perform the mercy *promised* to our fathers
And to remember His holy covenant,
[73] The oath which He swore to our father
Abraham:
[74] To grant us that we,
Being delivered from the hand of our enemies,
Might serve Him without fear,
[75] In holiness and righteousness before Him all
the days of our life.
[76] And you, child, will be called the prophet of
the Highest; For you will go before the face of
the Lord to prepare His ways."
(Luke 1:71-76)

John the Baptist and Jesus came in order to fulfill the decision that God made in the Abrahamic covenant. This is the same covenant that brings Israel into existence and bequeaths to her a peculiar role for the sake of world redemption. The book of Galatians also validates the Abrahamic covenant.

> [8] And the Scripture, foreseeing that God would justify the Gentiles by faith, preached the gospel to Abraham beforehand, *saying, "In you all the nations shall be blessed."* [9] So then those who *are* of faith are blessed with believing Abraham.
> *(Galatians 3:8-9)*

This verse tells us that the Abrahamic covenant was the first proclamation of the gospel. So those who are of faith are blessed with believing Abraham. If you have faith in this wonderful Jesus, then you are part of Abraham's covenant. You are blessed with him.

> [13] Christ has redeemed us from the curse of the law, having become a curse for us (for it is written, *"Cursed* is *everyone who hangs on a tree"*), [14] that the blessing of Abraham might come upon the Gentiles in Christ Jesus, that we might receive the promise of the Spirit through faith. *(Galatians 3:13-14)*

Why did Jesus become a curse for us? To fulfill the promise that God made to Abraham, that God would save the world and that the blessing of Abraham might come upon the Gentiles in Christ Jesus. That is, that we might receive the promise of the Spirit through faith. So our very reception of Jesus paves the way for all that God blessed us with in Abraham and his covenant.

Therefore, the New Testament scriptures validate, reinforce, and affirm the Abrahamic covenant which, at the same time, enforces Israel's role in history. This naturally challenges the notion that the Abrahamic covenant has been annulled and with it the role of Israel coupled with her destiny in the land of Canaan. This false thesis is known as Replacement Theology.

> [29] And if you *are* Christ's, then you are Abraham's seed, and heirs according to the promise. *(Galatians 3:29)*

Here again Paul says that if you belong to Jesus you have in fact received the blessings of the covenant that God made with Abraham 4,000 years ago. Abraham's covenant is still in force.

The New Testament is very clear about Israel. It affirms and validates the Abrahamic covenant. It affirms and validates the mission of the nation of Israel in history, and it affirms and validates the Old Testament concept of a coming kingdom and a world that will be regenerated because of a Jewish King who reigns from Jerusalem over the whole earth.

Natural Israel and Spiritual Israel

The New Testament validates the mysterious process by which the kingdom is established and will triumph. When God called Abraham He had the world in view. His focus was the nations.

> [13] For the promise that he would be the heir of the world *was* not to Abraham or to his seed through the law, but through the righteousness of faith. *(Romans 4:13)*

He would inherit the nations, not just the Jewish nation. The Jewish nation was to be the stepping stone to the nations.

One Family, One Flock

The purpose of God was to get a family, one family made up of all of those in different parts of the world who receive Jesus. That was the purpose of God and He has never changed it. He wanted to form one family of God, with one natural father, Abraham – a family that will be made up of children from every tribe, every tongue, and every nation.

What unites this family, whether they be Jew or Gentile, is their faith in Jesus the Messiah. That is what brings the family into existence and that is what the

29

promise of the Abrahamic covenant is. The New
Testament affirms this in John 10.

> [15] "As the Father knows Me, even so I know the
> Father; and I lay down My life for the sheep.
> [16]And other sheep I have which are not of this
> fold; them also I must bring, and they will hear
> My voice; and there will be one flock *and* one
> shepherd." *(John 10:15-16)*

There would be one flock and one shepherd. So
there is only one family of God and its natural father is
Abraham. Its great shepherd is Jesus and He says that
He has sheep from this flock – the Jewish flock –but He
has His eye on the nations, and "other sheep" who do
not belong to this flock, that is, the Gentiles.

Jesus says He is going to call them and make them
one flock in one sheep pen – not two sheep pens. He
says there will be one flock and there will be one
shepherd.

Natural Israel and Spiritual Israel

Now, the Apostle Paul introduced the concept of
natural Israel and spiritual Israel. It is a concept often
misunderstood. So let us look at what Paul teaches in
Romans.

> [28] For he is not a Jew who *is one* outwardly, nor
> *is* circumcision that which *is* outward in the
> flesh;
> [29] but *he is* a Jew who *is one* inwardly; and
> circumcision *is that* of the heart, in the Spirit,
> not in the letter; whose praise *is* not from men
> but from God. *(Romans 2:28-29)*

He says in effect that a true Jew is not one who has outward trappings that show that he is Jewish. A true Jew is one inwardly who has been circumcised in his heart by the Spirit of God.

Now this does not mean that Paul is discarding natural Israel. He is not removing from them their historical mission. He is just pointing out that the true Israel - or the true family of God – is made up of men and women who love Jesus.

He also knows that what he said is quite alarming: "A true Jew is not one outwardly." It is not a person who has been circumcised and has the outward national trappings of being Jewish. But a true Jew is one who has been circumcised by the Spirit of God, been regenerated and born again. He knows that he has just dropped a theological bombshell on them.

Moreover, he knows that this statement provokes a question in his reader's mind, the very question that might be provoked in your mind. The question is, "So where do the natural Jewish people fit in? Are they not Jews?" That is why in Romans 3:1 he asks the question that they have been asking: "What advantage then has the Jew?" Of course they are Jews. He is not denying their natural identity.

"But what about the person who is circumcised?" What is the purpose of circumcision - meaning the Jewish people? He just said that circumcision outwardly means nothing. So what is its purpose? What is the purpose of a natural Jew?

[1] What advantage then has the Jew, or what *is* the profit of circumcision? [2] Much in every way! Chiefly because to them were committed the oracles of God. [3] For what if some did not believe? Will their unbelief make the faithfulness of God without effect? [4] Certainly not! Indeed, let God be true but every man a liar…. *(Romans 3:1-4)*

Here he enforces the historical role given to the Jewish people, whether they were in belief or unbelief. Chiefly, they are the custodians of the Word of God. This is the nation that birthed redemptive products. This is the nation that by their unbelief gave us the death of Jesus.

Paul does not discard natural Israel. However, he does say that there is a natural Israel and there is a true Israel, or a spiritual Israel.

One Olive Tree

This brings us to Paul's teaching of the olive tree. The interesting thing about the olive tree is that you are only a part of this olive tree if you are a believer in Jesus. Whether you be Jew or Gentile you are only in this tree if you are a believer. If you do not believe, you are cut out of this tree. That is the teaching of Paul in Romans 11.

[17] And if some of the branches were broken off, and you, being a wild olive tree, were grafted in among them, and with them became a partaker of the root and fatness of the olive tree, [18] do not boast against the branches. But if you do boast,

remember that you do not support the root, but the root supports you.
[19] You will say then, "Branches were broken off that I might be grafted in." [20] Well *said.* Because of unbelief they were broken off, and you stand by faith. Do not be haughty, but fear. [21] For if God did not spare the natural branches, He may not spare you either. [22] Therefore consider the goodness and severity of God: on those who fell, severity; but toward you, goodness, if you continue in *His* goodness. Otherwise you also will be cut off. [23] And they also, if they do not continue in unbelief, will be grafted in, for God is able to graft them in again.
(Romans 11:17-23)

Don't boast against natural Israel that was broken off because they failed to embrace Jesus. Don't think that God is finished with their national destiny. If you do boast, remember that you do not support the root but the root supports you.

In other words, you are grafted into a tree of Jewish belief. On that tree are Moses, Abraham, David, Isaac, Jacob, and millions of Jewish people who in faith and trust came to God, believed the shadow of the cross, and He saved them.

You will say that branches were broken off that I might be grafted in. Well said. Because of unbelief they were broken off, so if you do not believe, you are not in the tree. We should not be haughty, but fear, for if God did not spare the natural branches, the natural Israel, He may not spare us either.

So just to recap, according to Paul, Jesus, and Abraham there is one family, not two families. Abraham is the father of one family made up of people from all over the world, including Jewish people.

The Bible does, however, teach this idea of two Israels. There is the natural Israel that does not believe and is outside of the tree, but that does not mean that God has removed from them the historical mission bequeathed to them in the Abrahamic covenant. That is why in Romans 11 Paul goes on to say:

> [28] Concerning the gospel they are enemies for your sake, but concerning the election they are beloved for the sake of the fathers.
>
> *(Romans 11:28)*

But there is only one tree. That tree is the real Israel – the spiritual Israel and you, by your faith in Jesus, have been grafted into it. There is only one tree. In this tree there are Jewish and Gentile believers in Christ, a "new man" (Ephesians 2:14-18).

In Galatians 6, Paul speaks of the "Israel of God" and includes the church in it. Some church expositors have incorrectly taken this passage to construe Replacement Theology.

This is simply not true! Rather, it is a reference to the one flock, to the one tree and to the one family which is and will be in eternity, the Israel of God. This view is consistent with the New Testament teaching on the nature of the family of God.

[15] For in Christ Jesus neither circumcision nor uncircumcision avails anything, but a new creation.
[16] And as many as walk according to this rule, peace and mercy *be* upon them, and upon the Israel of God.   *(Galatians 6:15-16)*

I say again this is the Israel of God – this is spiritual Israel. You can only be in this family if you have been born again, that is, regenerated by the Spirit of God and as a consequence, placed in the olive tree. It is only by exercising saving faith that we can remain in this tree. Sin, rebellion, and apostasy will result in our being cut off.

[22] Therefore consider the goodness and severity of God: on those who fell, severity; but toward you, goodness, if you continue in *His* goodness. Otherwise you also will be cut off.
                                        (Romans 11:22)

So it is interesting that this wonderful salvation is actually locked into the goodness of God. Do not ever think that anything in your Christian life is negative, even if it constitutes trials and difficulties. Some people complain at God and they have a "poor me" concept of their relationship with Him.

I think it offends God because He says He has saved us to do us good and that we should remain in His goodness. Morning by morning the God I serve is good. All His benefits to me are good. He only wants to do me good, even if this be through adversity.

Paul says, listen, if you do not remain in His goodness, He'll cut you off. I have seen people backslide when they have begun to question God. "God never helped me, God never did a thing for me. Look what happened to us." That is the beginning of the way out of the tree. We have to understand that we are only going to enter our spiritual Promised Land by encountering the blessings of a giant!

Butterflies are a perfect example of this. If you ever watch one of them in his cocoon stage, you will see him struggling to get out of the cocoon and you might be tempted to give the "little guy" a pull and help him. Sadly, that help would be his demise because the struggling process strengthens his wings so he can fly. If you help him, he will never fly.

My friends, the God you serve is good! He will take you to your spiritual Promised Land and He will deliberately put giants there because He wants to teach you how to fly. I am sorry there is no other way to learn to fly but through overcoming the giants. You have to struggle out of your cocoon so that the process brings you more fully into the goodness of God.

Restoration of Natural Israel

So the wonderful truth is that natural Israel still enjoys the privilege of being the custodian of the purpose of God. Moreover natural Israel, through a process of restoration in the Holy Land, will be grafted back into her own tree. Natural Israel will become the true Israel of God.

> [24] For if you were cut out of the olive tree which is wild by nature, and were grafted contrary to nature into a cultivated olive tree, how much

more will these, who *are* natural *branches,* be grafted into their own olive tree?

²⁵ For I do not desire, brethren, that you should be ignorant of this mystery, lest you should be wise in your own opinion, that blindness in part has happened to Israel until the fullness of the Gentiles has come in.

²⁶And so all Israel will be saved, as it is written: *"The Deliverer will come out of Zion, And He will turn away ungodliness from Jacob."*

(Romans 11:24-26)

Unbelieving Israel will remain out of the olive tree until the fullness of the Gentiles has come in. When this takes place, all Israel will be saved as it is written, the Deliverer will come out of Zion – the King will come!

So this return of the Jewish people, natural Israel, to their homeland is validated by the New Testament. It is an affirmation of the Abrahamic covenant.

The relocation of the Jewish people to the land of Canaan will result in the unraveling of the most incredible mystery that the world has ever seen. Namely, that when the last Gentile believes, according to God's election, then suddenly there will be an outpouring of the Spirit of God on natural Israel and she will be saved.

Natural Israel is destined to become spiritual, or real, Israel. This will bring our wonderful Messiah home to the Mount of Olives. I believe that He longs for that day to come. That is why Romans 11 teaches that the spiritual recovery of Israel will not only "trigger" the second coming of Messiah but it will also bring forth a blessing to the world that can only be likened to resurrection from the dead.

> [11] I say then, have they stumbled that they should fall? Certainly not! But through their fall, to provoke them to jealousy, salvation *has come* to the Gentiles. [12] Now if their fall *is* riches for the world, and their failure riches for the Gentiles, how much more their fullness!
> [13] For I speak to you Gentiles; inasmuch as I am an apostle to the Gentiles, I magnify my ministry, [14] if by any means I may provoke to jealousy *those who are* my flesh and save some of them. [15] For if their being cast away *is* the reconciling of the world, what *will* their acceptance *be* but life from the dead?
>
> *(Romans 11:11-15)*

Israel's failure in the natural state has brought great spiritual riches to the Gentile world. Imagine what is going to happen to us when natural Israel becomes spiritual Israel! Life from the dead!

When natural Israel is grafted back into the same tree, the King will come and these bodies of ours will be transformed and resurrected and those who lie in the dust of the earth who sleep in the Lord will come forth clothed in immortality. May God through our prayers hasten this day.

So the spiritual recovery of Israel will bring the King Messiah to the world. This is the teaching of Paul when he concludes his theological discourse on Israel - her call, destiny, and redemption.

[25] For I do not desire, brethren, that you should be ignorant of this mystery, lest you should be wise in your own opinion, that blindness in part has happened to Israel until the fullness of the Gentiles has come in.
[26] And so all Israel will be saved, as it is written: *"The Deliverer will come out of Zion, And He will turn away ungodliness from Jacob."*

(Romans 11:25-26)

There is only one tree, there is only one family, there is only one sheepfold. He says that as a consequence the Deliverer will come out of Zion and He will turn away ungodliness from Jacob. Why does he refer to Jacob and not Isaac or Abraham?

Jacob is a symbol of transformation. The God of Israel is going to transform natural Israel and make her a praise in the earth.

Do Not be Arrogant toward Natural Israel

Now, in the same great passage of Romans 11 the Apostle Paul gives a warning against being arrogant toward natural Israel. Those of us who have been grafted into the tree should not be arrogant toward the branches that have been taken out of the tree. They were broken off because of unbelief but still enjoy a national destiny and they are beloved for the sake of the Fathers.

[28] Concerning the gospel they are enemies for your sake, but concerning the election they are beloved for the sake of the fathers.

(Romans 11:28)

They are out of the tree. They do not believe. But concerning the election, that is God's choice of them in terms of their historical mission; they are beloved for the sake of their fathers.

> [17] And if some of the branches were broken off, and you, being a wild olive tree, were grafted in among them, and with them became a partaker of the root and fatness of the olive tree, [18] do not boast against the branches. But if you do boast, *remember that* you do not support the root, but the root supports you.
> [19] You will say then, "Branches were broken off that I might be grafted in." [20] Well *said.* Because of unbelief they were broken off, and you stand by faith. Do not be haughty, but fear. [21] For if God did not spare the natural branches, He may not spare you either. [22] Therefore consider the goodness and severity of God: on those who fell, severity; but toward you, goodness, if you continue in *His* goodness. Otherwise you also will be cut off. [23] And they also, if they do not continue in unbelief, will be grafted in, for God is able to graft them in again. [24] For if you were cut out of the olive tree which is wild by nature, and were grafted contrary to nature into a cultivated olive tree, how much more will these, who *are* natural *branches,* be grafted into their own olive tree?
>
> *(Romans 11:17-24)*

He says to the Gentile church that it should never get arrogant or boastful and never become disdainful of the Jewish people, the natural branches. If you say that branches were broken off that I might be grafted in, you are right. Because of unbelief they were broken off. You stand by faith so do not be haughty, but fear.

What a sad thing that through the centuries the Gentile church never took heed of these words. If anything, the Gentile church became arrogant, full of haughtiness, boastful, disdainful, and went even further.

The church accused them of being "Christ killers," accused them of deicide and of carrying a generational curse. It has been shocking and yet the Apostle Paul said that we should never do this. Now, let us look closely at verse 21.

^{21} For if God did not spare the natural branches, He may not spare you either.   *(Romans 11:21)*

Why does he say that? Notice the context – it is very interesting. He says, "One of the reasons why God might not spare you if you are in this redemptive tree is because of arrogance against natural Israel." That is the context. It certainly constitutes a wake-up call.

We know that the patience of God is incredible. But just as unforgiveness affects our redemptive relationship with God, so does an attitude of arrogance and disdain directed at the Jewish people who do not believe in Jesus.

Many fellowships are weak and powerless because of this sin. This is a serious warning. If you keep unforgiveness in your heart, there comes a time when God says He will not forgive you anymore. If you do not forgive your brother who sins against you, neither will God forgive you. Jesus said this plainly.

That is why we are called to lift up holy hands – hands that are open and do not bear any grudges, and do not hold any weapons. We lift up holy hands. We just want to be transparent. We just want to love God and do His will. Love covers a multitude of sins but there are people who are eaten up with hatred and unforgiveness against fellow Christians and against the Jews. The Bible says it affects their redemptive relationship with God. He will not forgive them.

I remember preaching a message like this in a house church. As I shared the Word of God, there was a man there who had suffered from a very serious back problem for years. This man hated a fellow believer and he would not deal with it. That night, however, the Spirit of God came on him and showed him his sin.

He confessed it to the Lord, and then stood before the group and confessed it publicly. The person he hated was not in the meeting so he made a plan immediately to reconcile with him. But that night in that meeting, as he wept, he said, "Lord, forgive me." In that very instant he was healed. God released him from his back pain.

Let me say again, that just as unforgiveness affects your redemptive relationship with God, so does an attitude of arrogance and disdain directed at the Jewish people. Many fellowships are weak and powerless because of this sin.

This is the context you see in Romans 11 where Paul encourages Christians not to be haughty but to fear. Not to be arrogant but to love the Jewish people. Then he said, "For if God did not spare the natural branches, he may not spare you either."

I am not saying that you lose your salvation. Of course you could if your sin becomes blatant anti-Semitism. I am saying that Christians who harbor unforgiveness, arrogance and hatred against the Jewish people incur the displeasure of God and are "playing with fire." If we keep on giving ourselves to these things, God, in the end, will not spare us. This is Paul's teaching in Romans 11.

We need therefore to guard our hearts in all aspects of life. As Christians we should not hate anybody. Jesus said, "Love your enemies, and pray for those who despitefully use you" (Matthew 5:44). So we have no excuses.

Nowhere does the New Testament give us the luxury of treating anyone with arrogance, certainly not the Jewish people, who, in their natural calling, have blessed us with our Messiah and His wonderful death. So we need to guard our hearts.

The National Spiritual Recovery of Israel

There is an interesting doctrine that I want to use to complete this exposition of Romans 11: the doctrine of firstfruit. To understand it in its rightful context, it is important that we read the verses in Romans 11 that lead up to its mention.

> [11] I say then, have they stumbled that they should fall? Certainly not! But through their fall, to provoke them to jealousy, salvation *has come* to the Gentiles. [12] Now if their fall *is* riches for the world, and their failure riches for the Gentiles, how much more their fullness!
> [13] For I speak to you Gentiles; inasmuch as I am an apostle to the Gentiles, I magnify my ministry, [14] if by any means I may provoke to jealousy *those who are* my flesh and save some of them. [15] For if their being cast away *is* the reconciling of the world, what *will* their acceptance *be* but life from the dead?
> [16] For if the firstfruit *is* holy, the lump *is* also *holy;* and if the root *is* holy, so *are* the branches.
> *(Romans 11:11-16)*

What does verse 16 mean? We will come back to Romans 11. But first, let us turn to James where the doctrine of firstfruit is mentioned again. James says that we who belong to Jesus are firstfruits.

¹⁸ Of His own will He brought us forth by the word of truth, that we might be a kind of firstfruits of His creatures.   *(James 1:18)*

If you turn to the book of I Corinthians, you find this doctrine mentioned again. Jesus is the firstfruits of the resurrection.

²⁰ But now Christ is risen from the dead, *and* has become the firstfruits of those who have fallen asleep.   *(1 Corinthians 15:20)*

So here we have the doctrine of firstfruit. The concept of firstfruit is that the firstfruit always guarantees a harvest. Jesus is the firstfruit of the resurrection, meaning millions are going to follow.

The firstfruit always guarantees a harvest. There is in the Bible a rather remarkable story about this in the Gospel according to Mark.

¹² Now the next day, when they had come out from Bethany, He was hungry. ¹³ And seeing from afar a fig tree having leaves, He went to see if perhaps He would find something on it. When He came to it, He found nothing but leaves, for it was not the season for figs. ¹⁴ In response Jesus said to it, "Let no one eat fruit from you ever again." And His disciples heard *it.*   *(Mark 11:12-14)*

²⁰ Now in the morning, as they passed by, they saw the fig tree dried up from the roots. ²¹ And Peter, remembering, said to Him, "Rabbi, look!

> The fig tree which You cursed has withered
> away." *(Mark 11:20-21)*

At first glance this seems a bit silly and even a bit crazy. This is the passion week and Jesus is living in Bethany with His friends, Mary, Martha and Lazarus. For some unknown reason He left the home that morning and He obviously did not have breakfast.

So Martha must have failed in her very busy duties that she normally discharged. You remember that Jesus said to her, "Martha, Martha, you are worried and busy about so many things but Mary has chosen the good portion that will not be taken from her," and that was to be at Jesus' feet (Luke 10:41).

Well, maybe Martha had learned the lesson and was having a quiet time with Jesus and forgot breakfast! That can be the only explanation as to why Jesus left home and was hungry.

Seeing from afar a fig tree, He went to see if perhaps He might find something on it. He wanted to find figs. When He came to it He found nothing but leaves. Why? It was not the season for figs. Okay, so why was He looking for figs? And, more important still, why would He say to it, "Let no one ever eat from you again?" Why?

Why would He curse this fig tree when it was not the season for figs? Well, if you go from Bethany toward Jerusalem and you ascend the Mount of Olives, you pass through the little village called Bethphage, which means "the house of the fig tree." Thus, as He got to Bethphage He saw all the fig trees.

47

Jesus knew that the time of the fig harvest is actually in September. That is when the tree would be laden with hundreds of figs. But He also knew that in March or April the tree should have its firstfruit. These first figs are absolutely the best-tasting and they are very nourishing.

So He rummaged through the leaves of the fig tree and could not find anything. When He did not find any firstfruit He knew that the tree was diseased. It was dying so He just speeded up the process: He cursed it. It would not bear a harvest.

If there is no firstfruit, there will be no harvest. If there are no figs in March or April, there will be no figs in September or October. The tree is diseased. That fig tree was used as a parable about those of that generation who were spiritually diseased.

However, the principle of the doctrine of firstfruit is there. That is, if there is firstfruit, there will be a harvest. This is why the Bible tells us that if you are in the church you are a kind of firstfruit. We are the first figs, and we are going to guarantee a harvest of figs from every nation.

In the millennium when Jesus comes and sits on His throne, there will be the saved nations. Millions and millions of people are going to get saved. These are the ones who will come up year by year to worship the Lord in Jerusalem (Zechariah 14:16).

The Bible says in the book of Revelation that the saved nations will enter the city and go out of the city with their kings that have come to worship. So we know there will be millions of people saved in the regeneration or messianic age. There is going to be a harvest from the nations, the likes of which we have never seen before.

> [24] And the nations of those who are saved shall walk in its light, and the kings of the earth bring their glory and honor into it. *(Revelation 21:24)*

But now we are the firstfruit. So we guarantee that from every tribe and every nation there is going to be a harvest in the messianic age.

Now let us return to Romans 11:16 where Paul talks about Israel and firstfruit. How do we know there is going to be a massive spiritual recovery of the Jewish people before the Messiah comes? Because their firstfruit is already on the tree; therefore, there will be a harvest. When the fullness of the Gentiles has come in, a kind of firstfruit of all His creatures, then all Israel is going to be saved. This will be a harvest like we have never seen.

How does Paul know that this will happen? This is his answer: because the firstfruit is holy. God has found firstfruit on Israel's fig tree so "the lump" – that is, the harvest – the big lump is going to be holy. Israel's fig tree is healthy and will bring forth a harvest. This is the teaching of Paul in Romans 11. There is coming a lump – a harvest of the nation of Israel – validated by the New Covenant scriptures – that is going to be unprecedented.

No wonder the final verses of Romans 11 give expression to Paul's eulogy of praise concerning the wonderful and mysterious ways of our God.

[33] Oh, the depth of the riches both of the wisdom and knowledge of God! How unsearchable are His judgments and His ways past finding out!
[34] *"For who has known the mind of the LORD?*
Or who has become His counselor?"
[35] *"Or who has first given to Him*
And it shall be repaid to him?"
[36] For of Him and through Him and to Him are all things, to whom be glory forever. Amen.

(Romans 11:33-36)

The most amazing thing about the story of Israel according to Paul is this: that a nation that is 4,000 years old, that passes into phases of belief and unbelief, nevertheless becomes the vehicle of world redemption. Strangely, in spite of their own rebellion, their weakness, and even being exposed to a power of darkness that constantly seeks to destroy them, the God of the Bible has accomplished His redemptive purposes for the world through them. Multitudes of men and women from every tribe and nation have become Abraham's children.

In the end, this nation that has been the vehicle of world redemption will herself enter into a period of unparalleled blessing and joy. Her long pilgrimage of suffering and darkness will have come to an end and for the first time since God called her into being, the world will understand that in fact, the nation of Israel was a gift to it. They will understand that through her every family of the earth has been blessed.

Four-Part
Biblical Zionism Series

The Basis of Christian Support for Israel

The basis of Christian support for Israel is found in God's promises to Abraham. The Abrahamic covenant declared God's love for the world and his establishment of a people through which to redeem the world. Israel's unique calling is still in force today and her return home to the land given to Abraham is evidence of that.

ISBN# 0-9765297-0-X

The Heart of Biblical Zionism

Clear biblical principles concerning God's dealings with Israel and the nations are the framework for an accurate interpretation of God's promises and calling on national Israel. Biblical Zionism is clearly defined and put in the correct theological context in this teaching.

ISBN# 0-9765297-1-8

The Great Covenants of the Bible

This exciting study of the four great covenants of the Bible also refutes Replacement Theology which teaches that the church has replaced Israel and Israel no longer has a unique call or destiny.

ISBN# 0-9765297-2-6

The New Testament and Israel

The New Testament validates a number of Old Testament doctrines concerning Israel. Foremost it affirms that God has not gone back on His promises to Israel.

ISBN# 0-9765297-3-4

and Another
Foundational Teaching
The Celebration of the Feast of Tabernacles

The Feast of Tabernacles is a celebration of the triumph of the kingdom of God and as such is now celebrated annually by Christians around the world.

ISBN# 0-9765297-4-2

INTERNATIONAL CHRISTIAN EMBASSY JERUSALEM

In the summer of 1980, the Israeli Parliament declared the city of Jerusalem to be the undivided, eternal capital of the State of Israel, established as such by King David almost 3,000 years earlier. Protest resounded across the international political spectrum, resulting in the closure of all but three national embassies that were in Jerusalem.

A number of Christians living in Israel were then hosting a Christian celebration during the Jewish Feast of Tabernacles. They sensed Israel's deep hurt over the withdrawal of the foreign embassies and felt the call of the Lord to open a Christian Embassy in this, the City of the Great King. They called it the International Christian Embassy Jerusalem and it represents Christians from around the world, speaking words of comfort and support to Israel. Ever since, the Embassy has provided a "servant's heart" ministry to the people of the land. Following are some of our major programs.

ALIYAH

Enables Christians to assist in the immigration and absorption of Jews from around the world. Projects have included helping more than 70,000 Jews to leave the former Soviet Union by either plane or bus to return to Israel. Our teams travel throughout numerous countries assisting and encouraging potential Jewish emigrants in the tedious process of relocating to Israel.

IMMIGRANT SUPPORT

Assists newly arriving immigrants from around the world with dental and medical needs, distribution of food vouchers and clothes, and emergency housing. A home has been established for the initial care of arriving immigrants as they face the challenges of a new life in Israel.

SOCIAL ASSISTANCE PROGRAM

Works with local Israeli agencies to provide financial, practical, and spiritual support to needy people.   Many joint projects have helped build bridges between different ethnic and religious communities, and have provided a witness to the providential love of God. Thousands of lives have been touched including Jews, Arabs, Christians, Muslims, Druze, Ethiopians, and Bedouins. Projects have included food, dental care, computer equipment, hearing aids, oxygen tanks, furniture, sheets, shoes, coats, an ambulance, a medical clinic, playground equipment, heaters, educational classes, and much more.

CHRISTIAN CELEBRATION DURING THE FEAST OF TABERNACLES

Brings thousands of Christians from over 100 nations to Jerusalem each year for a week of celebration, worship, and teaching during the only Jewish feast which instructs both Jew and Gentile to gather together before the Lord in Jerusalem to offer a sacrifice of thanksgiving.

INFORMATION MINISTRY

The ICEJ publishes a magazine "Word from Jerusalem" in different languages for worldwide distribution. Our website is a good source of information and the ICEJ's news service via the internet covers current issues affecting Israel's security and future. Quite often the Embassy's public affairs department issues statements and press releases on crucial matters. The Embassy also supplies thousands of audio and video teaching tapes explaining why Christians need to support God's purposes for Israel and Jerusalem.

INTERNATIONAL MINISTRY

The International Christian Embassy Jerusalem has representation in over 80 countries around the world. These branches regularly organize Israel Awareness events in their own countries, and plant seeds of love and support for Israel in local congregations. These include pro-Israel marches and petitions aimed toward governments and people of influence and they endeavor to challenge the nations from a biblical perspective concerning policies toward Israel.

This Foundational Teaching Series is also available in
Book
Audio CD
Audio Cassette Tape
Video
DVD

To schedule Rev. Hedding to speak, or to request further information about this series or the ICEJ contact us.

Name _____

Street Address _____

_____

City _____

State/Province _____

Zip Code/Postal Code _____

Country _____

Email Address _____

Phone Number _____

Produced and distributed by the ICEJ-USA.

International Christian Embassy Jerusalem

ISRAEL:
PO Box 1192
Jerusalem Israel 91010
email: icej@icej.org
www.icej.org

USA:
PO Box 39255
Washington, DC 20016
email: icejusa@icejusa.org
Phone: (202) 966-6992; Fax: (202) 966-6993

Notes

Notes